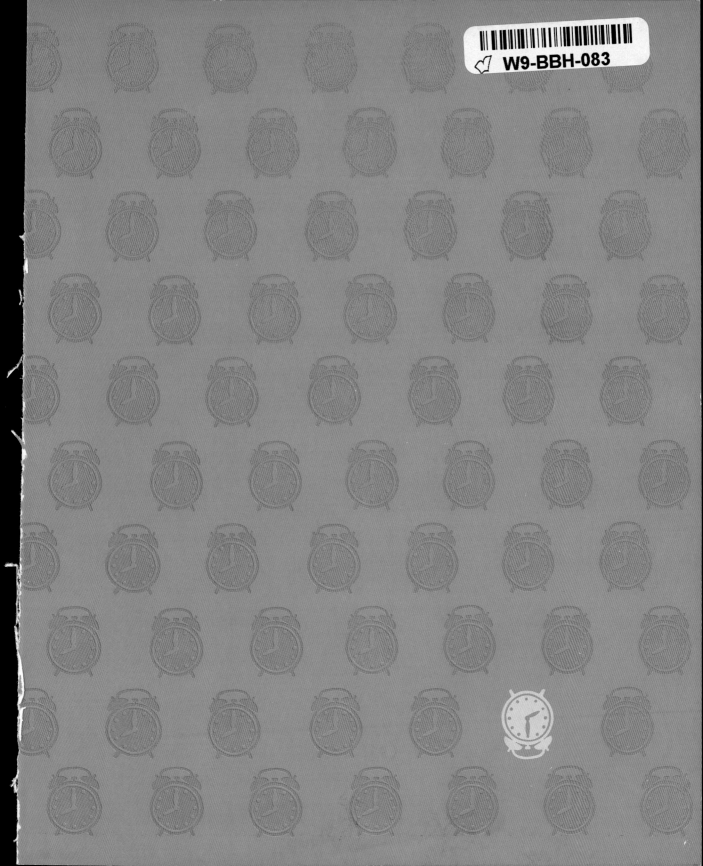

W9-BBH-083

A DORLING KINDERSLEY BOOK
Conceived, edited, and designed by DK Direct Limited

Note to parents

What's Inside? Everyday Things is designed to help young children understand the way some familiar everyday things work. It shows how a refrigerator keeps food cold, what goes on behind a clockface, and how a camera and film make photographs. It is a book for you and your child to read and talk about together, and to enjoy.

Editor Hilary Hockman
Designers Helen Spencer and Juliette Norsworthy
Typographic Designer Nigel Coath
US Editor Laaren Brown

Illustrators Paul Cooper and Jon Sayer
Photographers Matthew Ward and Steve Tanner
Written by Alexandra Parsons
Consultant Helen Birch
Design Director Ed Day
Editorial Director Jonathan Reed

First American Edition, 1992

10 9 8 7 6 5 4 3 2 1

Published in the United States by
Dorling Kindersley, Inc., 232 Madison Avenue
New York, New York 10016

Copyright © 1992 Dorling Kindersley Limited, London.

All rights reserved under International and Pan-American Copyright Conventions.
No part of this publication may be reproduced, stored in a retrieval system, or
transmitted in any form or by any means, electronic, mechanical, photocopying,
recording or otherwise, without the prior written permission of the copyright owner.
Published in Great Britain by Dorling Kindersley Limited, London.
Distributed by Houghton Mifflin Company, Boston, Massachusetts.

Library of Congress Cataloging-in-Publication Data
Everyday Things. – 1st American ed.
  p. cm. – (What's inside?)
  Summary: Examines the inner workings of various devices and
appliances found around the home, including the vacuum cleaner,
flashlight, and washing machine.
  ISBN 1-56458-134-9
  1. Household appliances, Electric – Juvenile literature.
[1. Household appliances, Electric. 2. Machinery.] I. Series.
TK7019.E74 1992
681.8 — dc20   92–52830 CIP AC

Printed in Italy

WHAT'S INSIDE?

EVERYDAY THINGS

DORLING KINDERSLEY, INC.
NEW YORK

FLASHLIGHT

If you carry a flashlight, you carry light with you. A flashlight is very useful on camping trips or if you are playing in the yard on a dark winter night. You often need one indoors, too, especially if you are looking for something in the back of a dark closet.

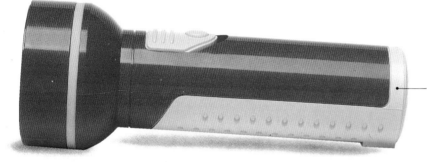

Flashlights are usually made of metal or tough plastic so they won't break easily.

You can see that the switch is on because all the metal strips are touching each other. Now electric power from the batteries can flow through to make the bulb glow.

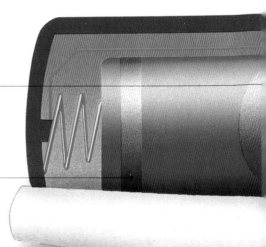

Batteries make electricity without wires and plugs! This flashlight needs two big batteries to make it work.

Long ago, people carried little oil lamps around for light. The lamps had wicks like candles.

The bulb is screwed into a metal bulb-holder. The holder is connected to the batteries by metal strips.

The transparent lens, made of plastic or glass, protects the bulb. The shiny reflector behind the bulb makes the light seem brighter.

This is the on/off switch. If you leave it on, the batteries will get used up and the light will slowly fade and go out.

WASHING MACHINE

Thank goodness for washing machines! They take all the hard work out of washing clothes. To get clothes clean, you have to push the soapy water through the clothes so the water will take the dirt away, and that's what a washing machine does.

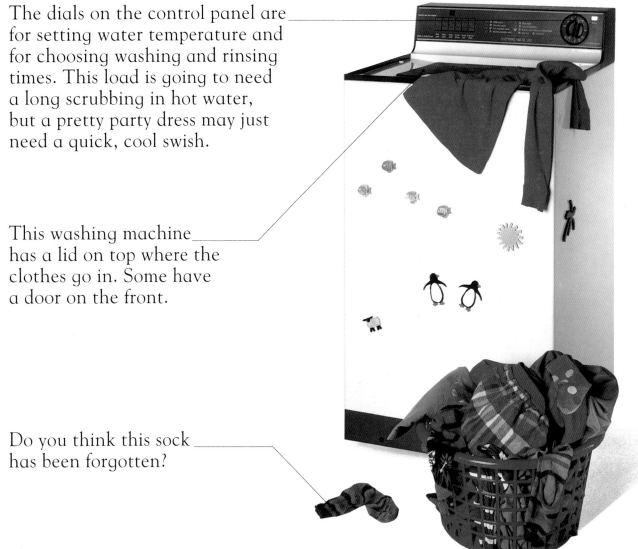

The dials on the control panel are for setting water temperature and for choosing washing and rinsing times. This load is going to need a long scrubbing in hot water, but a pretty party dress may just need a quick, cool swish.

This washing machine has a lid on top where the clothes go in. Some have a door on the front.

Do you think this sock has been forgotten?

Early washing machines had to be filled from the pump, turned by hand, and emptied with a hose.

Clean water comes in through these pipes.

Dirty water comes out here. If the washing machine has done its job, the water will be dirty and the clothes will be clean!

Clothes are washed and rinsed in this drum. It has lots of holes in it so water can swirl in and out.

The paddle swishes the clothes from side to side.

At the end of the wash cycle, the motor turns the drum round and round very fast to spin all the rinse water out.

STEAM IRON

Clothes come out of the washing machine crumpled and rumpled. Ironing gets rid of all the creases and makes clothes look good and feel comfortable to wear.

This dial controls how hot the soleplate gets. The tougher the fabric, the hotter the iron needs to be. Delicate fabrics will burn or melt if the iron is too hot.

This is the soleplate. It is made of metal and gets very hot, so don't touch!

The handle is made of special plastic that does not get hot.

Once upon a time..."smoothing irons," as they were called, were heated up on a charcoal fire. Ironing was a hot and dangerous business.

The water drips through this valve into the hot steam chamber, where it is turned into steam.

Water is poured in here. It turns into steam inside the iron, and the steam comes out of little holes in the soleplate.

Steam comes out here to dampen the fabric.

The electric element heats the soleplate.

It is easier to press clothes smooth if they are damp.

CLOCK

This alarm clock works by clockwork. It doesn't need electricity or batteries. You just have to remember to wind it up every day. When you wind a clock, you tighten a spring. As the spring unwinds, it moves cogwheels with little teeth that move the hands round and round.

This is the hammer that hits the alarm bells that make the noise that wakes you up in time to get to school.

Here's the big hand. The big hand takes one hour to go around the clockface...

You use this hand to set the alarm.

...and here's the little hand. It takes twelve hours to go around.

Once upon a time...people told the time by looking at shadows cast by the sun. As long as the sun is shining, a sundial is accurate, but of course it doesn't work at night, and it hasn't got a bell to wake you up!

This key winds the spring.

This lever sets off the alarm. When the little hand reaches the time set on the dial, the lever releases the hammer. Don't forget to set the alarm before you go to sleep!

These cogwheels turn the hands of the clock

As the spring unwinds it makes the cogwheels turn.

CAMERA

To take a photograph, you need a camera. A camera "sees" light just like your eyes do. The light that goes into a camera makes a picture on a layer of chemicals on a sheet of film. This picture stays hidden on the film until you take it to be developed and printed.

This little wheel winds the film. When you've taken one picture, you wind onto a new piece of film to take another.

Click! When you press this button, you take a picture!

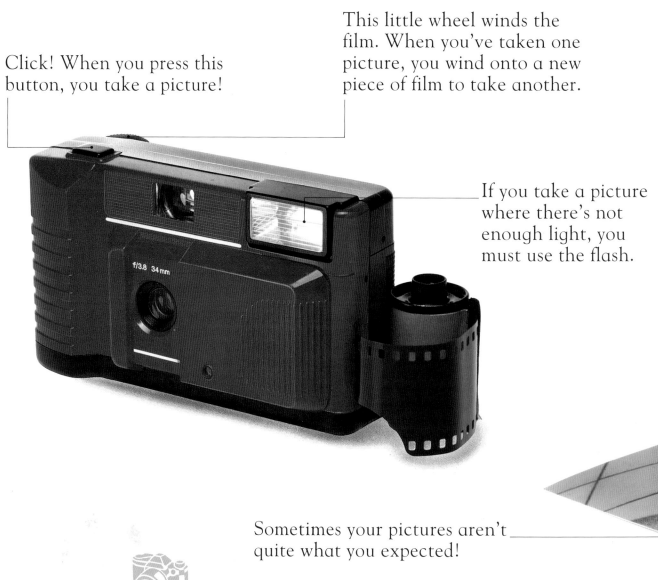

If you take a picture where there's not enough light, you must use the flash.

Sometimes your pictures aren't quite what you expected!

When cameras and film were first invented, it took a very long time for the light to make a picture. People had to sit absolutely still for ten minutes or more.

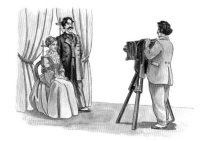

This is the shutter. When you press the button, its little sections spring open and shut again very quickly.

This window is called the viewfinder. Look through it to see the picture you are going to take.

When the shutter opens, it lets light from the object in through this curved piece of glass called a lens. The light makes the picture on the film.

The film is stretched across the back of the camera on rollers.

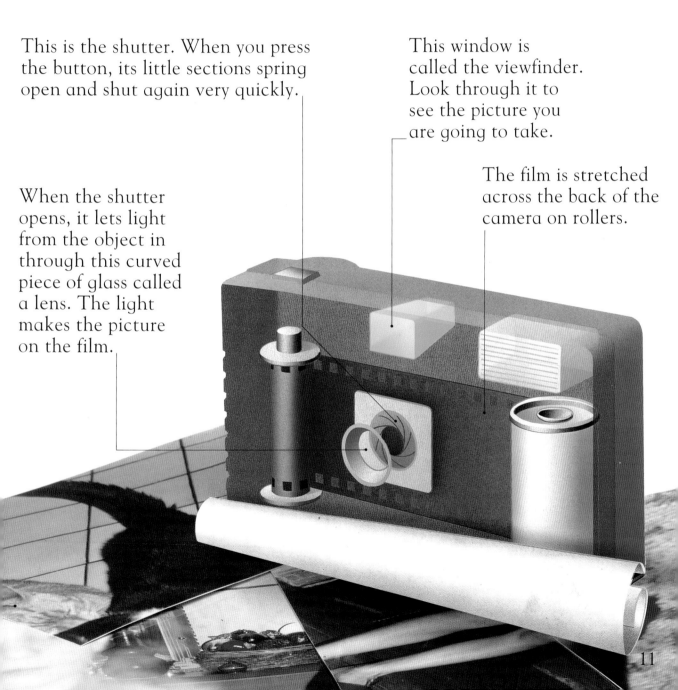

REFRIGERATOR

We keep fresh food in a cold refrigerator to keep it from going bad. Tiny invisible living things called bacteria are everywhere. If food is left lying around in warm air, the bacteria in it grows and makes the food go bad. Cold slows the growing bacteria down. Freezing stops them completely.

Can you think of foods that don't need to go in the refrigerator? Canned foods like beans can be kept in a cupboard because no bacteria can get inside the can – until you open it.

The freezer compartment is much colder than the rest of the refrigerator. In here, water turns into ice and fruit juice into ice pops. Yum!

The inside of a refrigerator is covered with white plastic. It is easy to keep sparkling clean.

Close that door quickly! Refrigerator doors have rubber seals around the outside to make sure no cold air escapes and no warm air gets in.

Once upon a time...refrigerators were just cabinets that held big blocks of ice. They looked like pieces of furniture.

Refrigerators cool food by taking warmth away from the air. Inside these pipes is a special liquid. As the liquid goes through the pipes, it turns into a gas and draws the heat away.

This part is called the condenser. It turns the gas back into a liquid.

As the gas turns to liquid again, it lets off the heat it has taken in. You can feel warm air coming from the grille at the front – and now you know why!

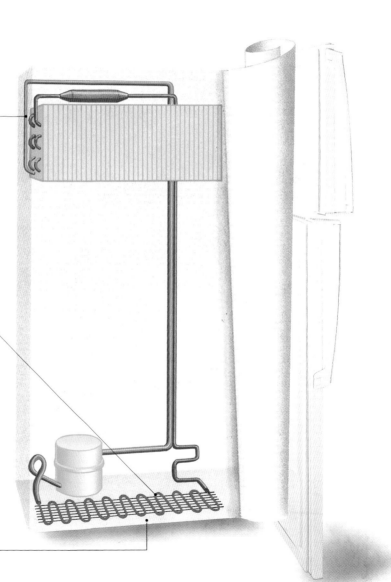

PERSONAL STEREO

On this small tape player you can listen to your favorite music through earphones, without disturbing anyone else. Be careful not to turn the volume too high – you could hurt your ears!

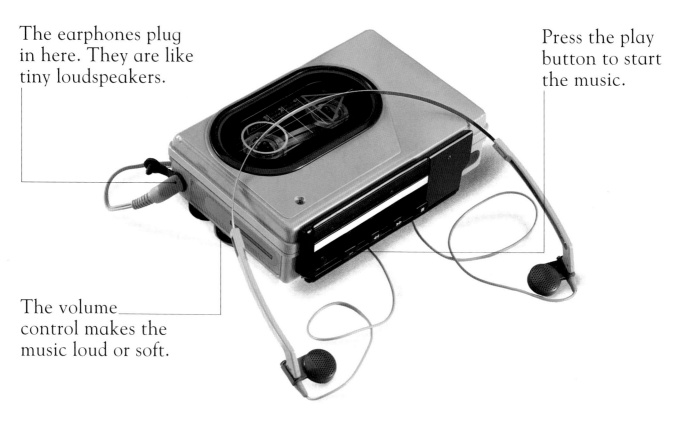

The earphones plug in here. They are like tiny loudspeakers.

Press the play button to start the music.

The volume control makes the music loud or soft.

Once upon a time...only kings, queens, and the nobility had music wherever they went.

The drive motor turns a spindle that moves a little wheel in the center of the tape spool. The wheel turns the tape.

Inside the cassette, the tape winds from one reel to the other.

When the play button is pressed, this playing head moves forward to touch the tape. The tape sends its signal to the head.

Music for one "side" is recorded along the top of the tape, and for the other "side," along the bottom.

The head passes the signal down the wires to the earphones so you hear the music on the tape.

15

VACUUM CLEANER

Dust gets everywhere. It is floating around in the air all the time. It settles on carpets and furniture, making everything look grubby. That's where the vacuum cleaner comes in. A quick whiz around, and the house looks clean and fresh.

A vacuum cleaner works by sucking in dust. All you have to do is point the hose in the right place! The cleaning head is at the end of a long, bendy pipe.

The vacuum cleaner is on wheels so it can be pulled along easily.

This is the electric cord.

A vacuum cleaner will suck up anything that will go down the tube. Watch out for toys that haven't been put away!

Early vacuum cleaners needed two people to make them work. One person pumped the air while the other used the hose to suck up dust.

The electric motor turns the fan.

The fan inside spins around so fast it pushes air out of the way, leaving a space with no air called a vacuum. Dusty air rushes up the flexible tube to fill the space.

The dusty air is sucked into this paper bag... along with the toys. They nearly got lost forever! Air can go in and out of the bag. The dust and toys stay in the bag, but clean air comes out.